MARTIAL ARTS
KARATE

by Tim O'Shei

Reading Consultant:
Barbara J. Fox
Reading Specialist
North Carolina State University

Content Consultant:
Cleveland Baxter
Chairman, United States National Karate-Do Federation
Referee Committee
Colorado Springs, Colorado

Capstone
press®
Mankato, Minnesota

Blazers is published by Capstone Press,
151 Good Counsel Drive, P.O. Box 669, Mankato, Minnesota 56002.
www.capstonepress.com

Library of Congress Cataloging-in-Publication Data
O'Shei, Tim.
    Karate / by Tim O'Shei.
    p. cm. — (Blazers. Martial arts)
    Summary: "Discusses the history, techniques, ranks, and competitions of
karate" — Provided by publisher.
    Includes bibliographical references and index.
    ISBN-13: 978-1-4296-1961-5 (hardcover)
    ISBN-10: 1-4296-1961-9 (hardcover)
    1. Karate — Juvenile literature. I. Title.
GV1114.3.O84 2009
796.815'3 — dc22   2007052202

Essential content terms are **bold** and are defined on the spread where they first appear.

Editorial Credits
Abby Czeskleba, editor; Ted Williams, designer; Jo Miller, photo researcher;
    Sarah L. Schuette, photo shoot direction; Marcy Morin, scheduler

Photo Credits
All principle photography by Capstone Press/Karon Dubke except:
Getty Images Inc./AFP/Pekka Sakki, 24; The Image Bank/Chris Cole, 7
iStockphoto/Nancy Kennedy, 5; slobo mitic, 17
Zuma Press/Courtesy of Cannon Group, 27

The Capstone Press Photo Studio thanks the members of the National Karate School
in Rochester, Minnesota, for their assistance with photo shoots for this book.

1 2 3 4 5 6 13 12 11 10 09 08

TABLE OF CONTENTS

CHAPTER 1
OKINAWA

During the early 1600s, the **samurai** took over the Ryukyuan (RI-yoo-kee-an) Kingdom. The people of the kingdom needed to defend themselves against the samurai's swords. The people used farming tools like *bo* and *kama*.

MARTIAL ARTS FACT

The Ryukyuan Kingdom was located on an island. That island is now called Okinawa.

samurai — Japanese warriors who fought in battles between the years 500 and 1877

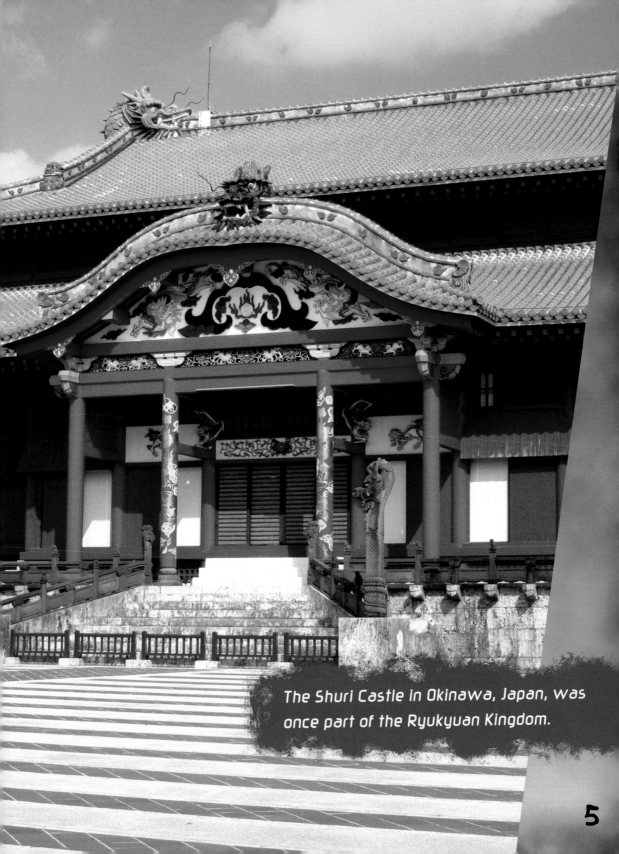

The Shuri Castle in Okinawa, Japan, was once part of the Ryukyuan Kingdom.

People also fought the samurai with punches, kicks, and blocks. They were using an early form of karate. Today, karate is one of the most popular martial arts.

Karate means "empty hand."

More than 50 million
people practice karate.

CHAPTER 2
PRACTICING KARATE

Karate fighters wear a uniform called a *gi*. They also wear padded gloves and shoes during matches.

MARTIAL ARTS FACT

Karate fighters are called *karateka*.

gi — the pants and jacket worn by a karate fighter

Karate fighters turn their hips to get full power behind their kicks. During competition, fighters jump back and forth. This footwork helps fighters move quickly.

Karate fighters learn kicks, strikes, and punches from a **sensei**. Students bow to their sensei before and after class. They bow to show respect.

Karate fighters sometimes practice with weapons. These weapons include the bo and kama. Skilled karate fighters may also use swords and spears in their **kata**.

MARTIAL ARTS FACT

Fighters use some of the same weapons used by the Okinawans in the 1600s.

kata — a set of movements used in karate

Karate fighters practice with a bo (left) and kama (right).

15

CHAPTER 3
MASTERING KARATE

Beginning students wear white belts. They have the rank of *kyu*. Students earn different colored belts as they improve. There are 10 kyu levels. A first kyu is the highest level.

MARTIAL ARTS FACT

There are seven belt colors in karate. They include white, yellow, and orange. Belts can also be green, blue, brown, or black.

After mastering the 10 kyu levels, a student becomes a *dan*. Dan fighters wear black belts. A 10th dan level is the highest rank in karate.

KARATE DIAGRAM

COMPETITION AREA

REFEREE
National Karate
BLACK BELT
PADDED GLOVE
PADDED SHOE

CHAPTER 4

KARATE COMPETITIONS

Fighters use their skills in karate matches. Every fighter belongs to a certain **weight class**. A referee awards points for punches and kicks. Fighters can earn one, two, or three points for each move.

MARTIAL ARTS FACT

The first fighter to lead by eight points wins the match.

weight class — a group of karate fighters who are the same weight; fighters in the same weight class compete one-on-one against each other.

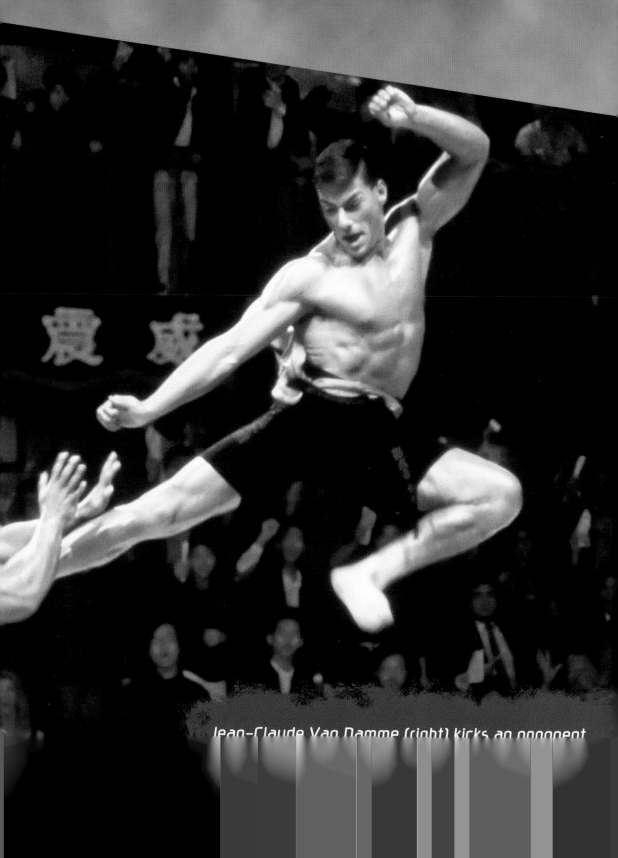

Jean-Claude Van Damme (right) kicks an opponent

23

In 2006, the 18th World Karate Championships were held in Tampere, Finland. Karate fighters from 81 countries attended the tournament. The world championships are held every two or three years.

MARTIAL ARTS FACT

Fighters from 33 countries attended the first World Karate Championships in 1970.

Karate fighters are also seen in movies. Actor Jean-Claude Van Damme has a black belt. Many of his movies have hard punches and high-flying kicks. After all, karate is all about exciting action!

MARTIAL ARTS FACT

The Karate Kid from 1984 is one of the most famous karate movies.

KARATE KICK!

29

GLOSSARY

bo (BOH) — a long wooden staff first used to herd livestock; a karate fighter uses a bo to strike different areas of another fighter's body.

defend (di-FEND)—to stop an attack

gi (GEE) — the pants and jacket worn by a karate fighter

kama (KAMA) — a bladed weapon with a wooden handle first used to cut rice and grass; a karate fighter uses kama to strike another fighter or block punches and kicks.

kata (KAH-tah) — a set of movements used in karate

popular (POP-yuh-lur) — liked or enjoyed by many people

referee (ref-uh-REE) — a person who makes sure athletes follow the rules of a sport

samurai (SAH-muh-rye) — Japanese warriors who fought in battles between the years 500 and 1877

sensei (SEN-say) — the Japanese word for teacher

weight class (WATE KLAS) — a group of karate fighters who are the same weight; fighters in the same weight class compete one-on-one against each other.

READ MORE

Buckley, Thomas. *Karate.* Kids' Guide to Martial Arts. Chanhassen, Minn.: Child's World, 2004.

Cook, Harry. *Karate.* Martial Arts. Milwaukee: Gareth Stevens, 2005.

Rielly, Robin L. *Karate for Kids.* Tuttle Martial Arts for Kids. Boston: Tuttle, 2004.

INTERNET SITES

FactHound offers a safe, fun way to find Internet sites related to this book. All of the sites on FactHound have been researched by our staff.

Here's how:
1. Visit *www.facthound.com*
2. Choose your grade level.
3. Type in this book ID **1429619619** for age-appropriate sites. You may also browse subjects by clicking on letters, or by clicking on pictures and words.
4. Click on the **Fetch It** button.

FactHound will fetch the best sites for you!

INDEX